Helping Children See Jesus

ISBN: 978-1-64104-025-9

Discovering God's Ways
Old Testament Volume 17:
Joshua Part 2

Author: Arlene S. Piepgrass
Computer Graphic Artist: Samuel Laterza
Page Layout: Morgan Melton, Patricia Pope

© 2021 Bible Visuals International
PO Box 153, Akron, PA 17501-0153
Phone: (717) 859-1131
www.biblevisuals.org

All rights reserved. No part of this publication may be reproduced, stored in a retrieval system or transmitted in any form by any means, electronic, mechanical, photocopy, recording or otherwise, without the prior permission of the publisher, except as provided by USA copyright law.

RELATED ITEMS

To access related items (such as activities, memory verse posters and translated texts) please visit our web store at www.biblevisuals.org and enter 2017 in the search box on the page.

FREE TEXT DOWNLOAD

To access a FREE printable copy of the teaching text (PDF format) in English or other available languages, enter 2017 in the search box. Add the item to your cart, and use coupon code XTACSV17 at checkout. Once your order is processed you will receive an email with a link to the free download.

STUDENT ACTIVITES

These are included with the FREE printable copy of the English teaching text for this story. See the directions under Free Text Download (above) to access them.

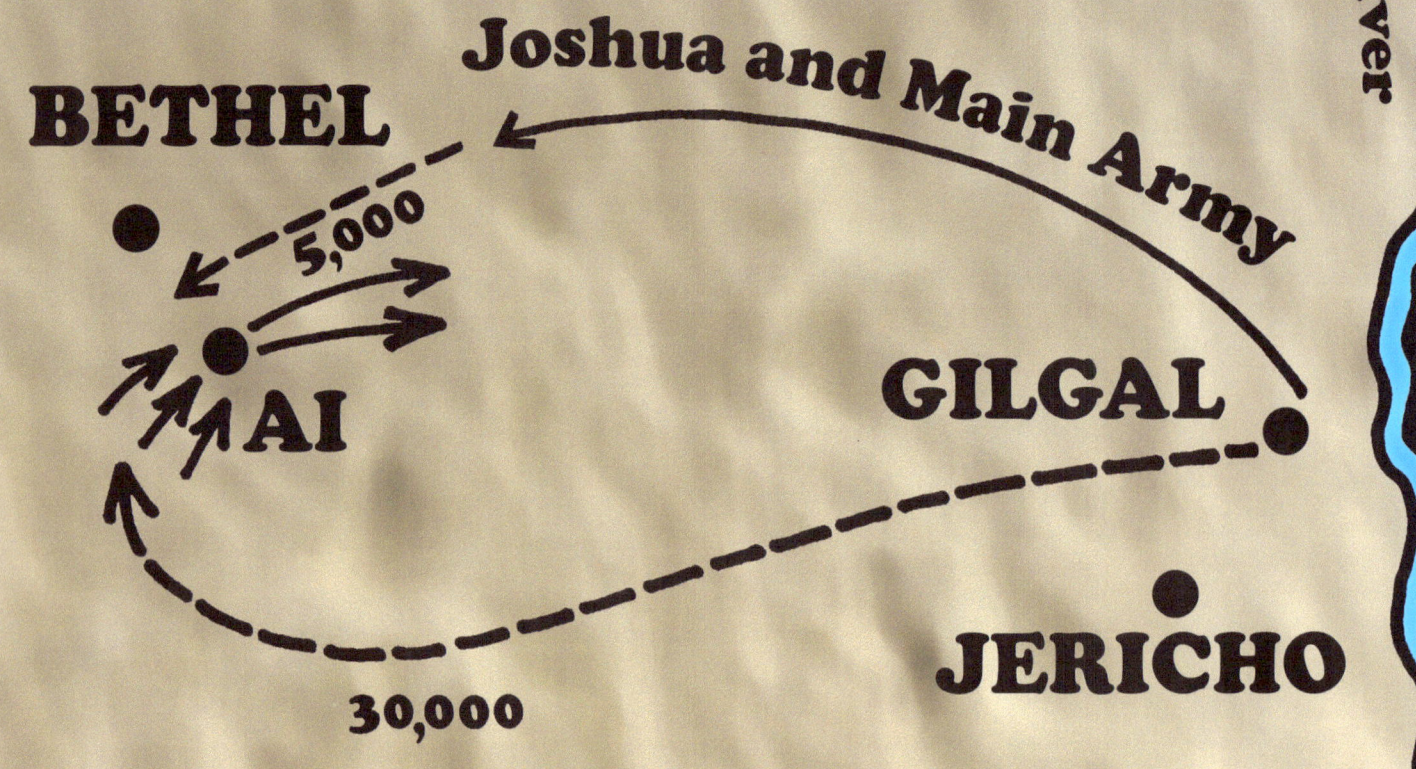

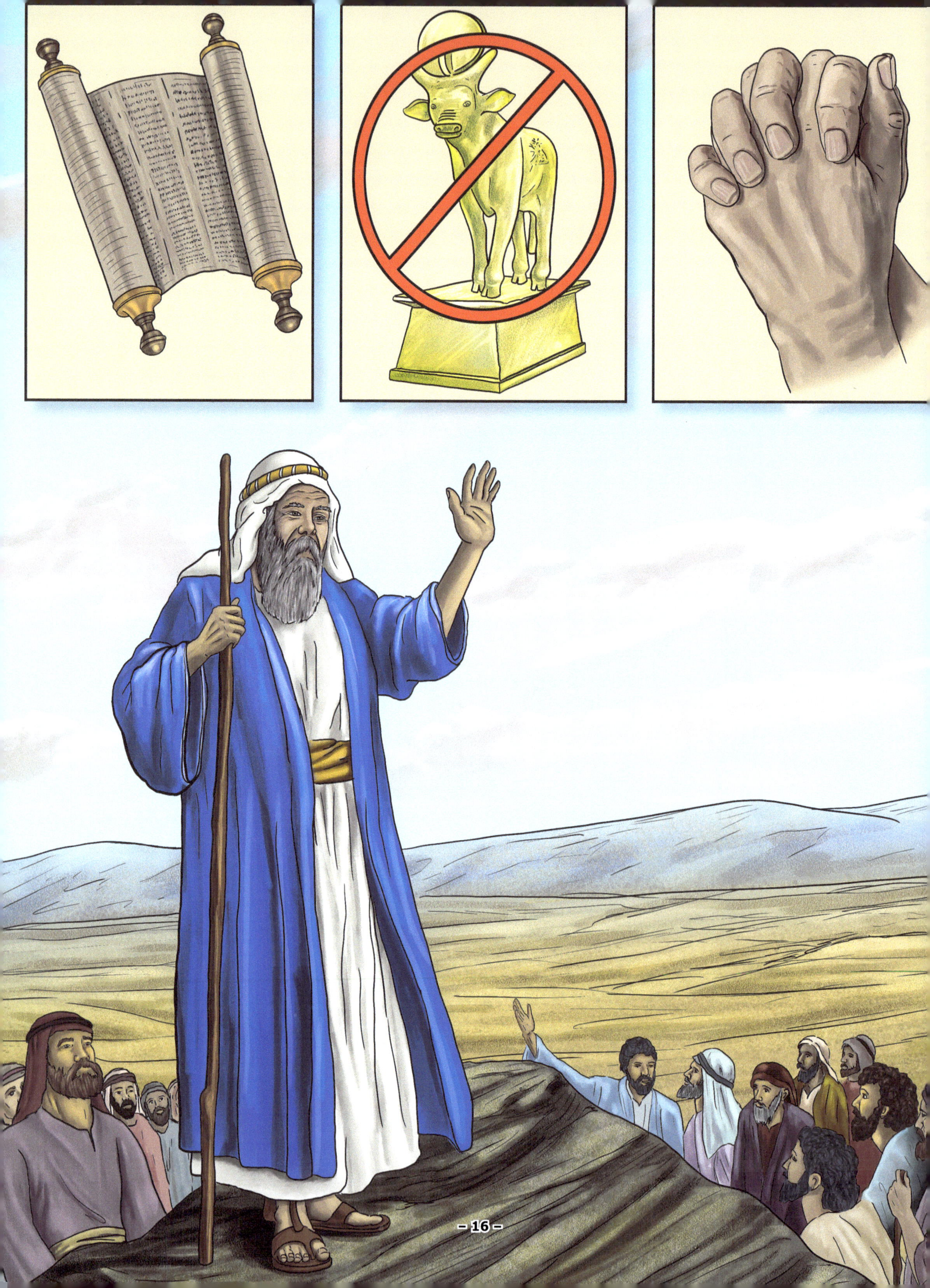

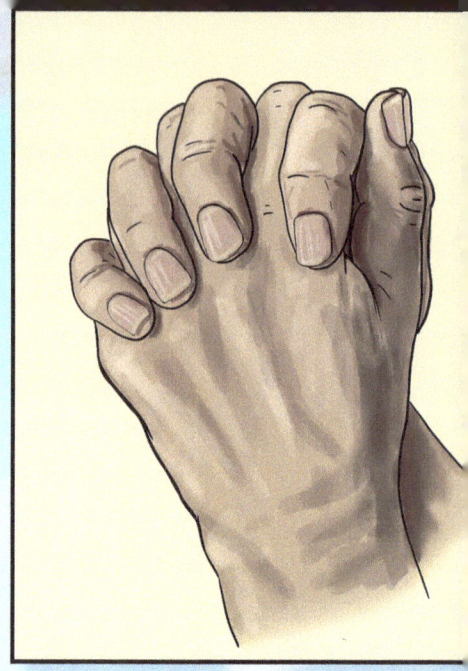

"Fear the LORD, and serve Him in sincerity and in truth . . ." Joshua 24:14a

Lesson 1
SIN AND DEFEAT

NOTE TO THE TEACHER

To be most effective, this volume on Joshua should be taught immediately after teaching Old Testament Volume 16.

The book of Joshua records the Israelites' conquest of Canaan. The experiences of the people of Israel teach us spiritual lessons for our own lives (1 Corinthians 10:11). The sin and defeat at Ai (see Joshua 7) are solemn warnings for us. It was the only battle the Israelite people lost in their seven–year conquest of Canaan. Because of one man's sin, God could not bless them.

The principles are as true today as in the days of Joshua. We must beware of crying to God for help if we are hiding sin in our lives.

1. Nothing can be kept secret from God (Proverbs 15:3). He sees everything. "Be sure your sin will find you out" (Numbers 32:23).
2. Others are affected by our sin. (See 1 Corinthians 12:26.) "A little leaven leaveneth the whole lump" (1 Corinthians 5:6).
3. "Pride goes before destruction" (Proverbs 16:18). The success at Jericho caused the Israelites to be self-confident. They forgot that they had not won by their own strength. *God* had given them the victory. Because of self-confidence they neglected prayer and, as a result, suffered defeat.

Scripture to be studied: Joshua 7; verses cited in lesson.

The *aim* of the lesson: To show that no sin can be hidden from God.

What your students should *know*: Sin breaks our fellowship with God and hurts other people.

What your students should *feel*: The awfulness of being guilty before God.

What your students should *do*: Confess to God any secret sin and obtain His forgiveness.

Lesson outline for the teacher's and students' notebooks:
1. Achan's sin (Joshua 7:1, 21).
2. Joshua's negligence (Joshua 7:2-3).
3. Israel's defeat at Ai (Joshua 7:4-15).
4. Confession and judgment (Joshua 7:19-26).

The verse to be memorized:

Fear the LORD, and serve Him in sincerity and in truth.
(Joshua 24:14a)

THE LESSON

Jericho was a heap of ruins. Everyone who had lived there was dead. That is, everyone except Rahab and her family who were rescued (Joshua 6:22-25). All the animals were dead. The houses were burned. Only those things made of silver and gold or brass and iron were saved. What had happened? (*Teacher*: With questions review the events of Joshua 6. Use illustrations from Old Testament Volume 16, Lesson 4.)

1. ACHAN'S SIN
Joshua 7:1, 21

Did you ever steal anything? Did it make you happy? (*Teacher*: Mention your own experience of stealing.) Stealing is sin. We thought no one saw us steal. But God sees everything!

Achan was a soldier in the army of Israel. He was with the others who had marched around the city of Jericho 13 times. With all the Israelite people, he shouted when Joshua gave the signal. And he saw the walls of Jericho fall outward to the ground just as God had promised.

In obedience to the Lord, Achan and the other soldiers rushed into the city to destroy everyone. The soldiers began to burn the houses and everything which belonged to the wicked people of Jericho. God had ordered this, too.

But Achan did not help the others. Instead, he stopped to look at the exquisite belongings of the rich people. As he looked, he wanted some of the things for himself!

The warnings Joshua had given flashed through his mind. "Do not take *anything* for yourselves. You will see beautiful things you would like to have. Do not yield to temptation. *Everything* must be destroyed. These are God's orders. If you disobey, everyone will suffer."

Achan quickly erased these thoughts from his mind. He gazed at an expensive robe thinking, *It is magnificent. How handsome I would look in it!* Achan looked all around. No one was watching. Quickly he hid the robe under his uniform. As he did so, something else caught his attention. *Look at that stack of silver coins*, he thought. *And the wedge of gold. If I had all that money I would be rich!*

Achan grabbed the silver and gold and, tiptoeing from one shadow to another, rushed to his tent.

Showing the coins and robe to his family, he whispered, "Look what I found! Hurry, help me dig a hole here inside the tent to hide them. Do not tell anyone! No one will ever know I took them from Jericho."

Show Illustration #1

Quickly he buried the treasures and covered the hole. Then Achan reported for duty as if nothing had happened.

What was wrong with Achan's actions and attitudes? (Let students discuss. *Achan deliberately disobeyed God. Achan was selfish. He wanted what did not belong to him. Achan forgot that God sees everything. Achan forgot God's warning that others would suffer because of his sin.*)

2. JOSHUA'S NEGLIGENCE
Joshua 7:2-3

The shouts of victory reechoed in the camp of Israel. News of the overthrow of Jericho spread throughout the whole land of Canaan. Everyone there was dreadfully afraid of Joshua and the Israelite army (Joshua 6:27).

Joshua began to make plans for the next attack. Ai was a small city north of Jericho. (Indicate on map.) It had to be destroyed before the people of Israel could move farther into Canaan.

Show Illustration #2

Joshua chose a few of his special soldiers. He instructed them, "Go up to the city of Ai. See how strong the city is. Let me know how large an army they have so we can make our battle plans."

When the soldiers returned, they were enthusiastic. "We can easily conquer Ai," they reported. "They have only 2,000 soldiers in their army. Using only 2,000 or 3,000 of our men we can quickly defeat the army of Ai."

"Good," Joshua agreed immediately. "I shall send 3,000."

Do you wish you could have tapped Joshua on the shoulder saying, "You forgot something!" What had Joshua forgotten? (Stimulate response.) He forgot to ask God for guidance. He was trusting his own wisdom.

Do you recall what Joshua did before Israel began their march around Jericho? (Review Joshua 5:13-6:5, Old Testament Volume 16, Lesson 4.) He worshiped the Lord. He talked to God about the difficult task. God told him exactly what to do and promised to give victory to the people of Israel.

Now Joshua was acting as if the Israelites could defeat their enemies without God's help. The victory at Jericho made him proudly confident of his own power. Joshua depended on the reports of the soldiers instead of asking God to reveal His plan for attacking Ai.

If only Joshua had remembered that his army had not conquered Jericho alone. It was God who gave the victory!

3. ISRAEL'S DEFEAT AT AI
Joshua 7:4-15

The army of Israel marched toward Ai with great assurance. The Bible does not tell us what they said among themselves. Could it have been like this?

"The people of Ai surely have heard what we did to Jericho!" they boasted to each other. "They must be terrified. Today their city will also be destroyed and they all will die!"

But when the Israelite army approached the city, the army of Ai rushed out fiercely. Joshua's soldiers were so frightened that they turned and raced back to their own camp. And 36 of the Israelite soldiers were killed in the retreat. Something had gone wrong.

How do you think the other Israelites felt when they saw their soldiers scrambling back defeated? (Let students respond. Read the last part of Joshua 7:5 comparing it with Joshua 2:9-11.)

Joshua was bewildered. He and the Israelite leaders tore their clothes and put dirt on their heads. These were signs of their grief.

Show Illustration #3

Then they fell on their faces before the Ark of the Lord and stayed there until evening. (Remember: God met with His people above the Ark.) Questions of despair tumbled out of Joshua's mouth. "O Lord, what has happened? Did You bring us across the Jordan River to be killed by these people? Lord God, what am I going to do now that our army has been defeated? Everyone in Canaan will hear about this. They will surround us and kill all of us! And, Lord, what will happen to the glory and honor of Your great name?"

God commanded severely, "Joshua, get up! This is not the time to pray. The Israelites have sinned. Someone has stolen from Me. He has taken from Jericho something which I said *not* to be taken. And he has hidden it among his own possessions. This is why Israel was defeated. This is why your men are running away from their enemies. I shall not help you *unless* you take care of this sin."

If Joshua had remembered to pray before attacking Ai, God would have told him this at that time. Then the defeat and discouragement could have been avoided.

Joshua had not seen anyone stealing anything from Jericho. He had not seen anyone hiding stolen goods. How could he know who was guilty?

God explained, "Tomorrow I shall show you who is responsible. Command the Israelites to walk before you by tribes. I shall point out the guilty tribe. That tribe must walk before you by families and I shall make known the guilty family. Then each member of that family must come one by one and I shall reveal the guilty man."

"How is he to be punished?" asked Joshua.

"The guilty man and all he owns must be destroyed by fire," God replied. "Because he disobeyed, he has brought trouble to *all* the Israelites."

The next morning Joshua followed God's orders. It took a long time. How would you have felt if you had been standing there waiting your turn to walk past Joshua? (Let students suggest emotions: fear, tension, questions such as "Did I do something wrong? Am I guilty?")

One man knew who was guilty. Who was that? (*Achan*) How do you think he felt? (Allow discussion.) Oh how his heart pounded! When he stole the forbiden things from Jericho, he thought no one saw him. He forgot that God sees *everything*. He presumed his sin would never be discovered. But he could not hide from God.

Achan moved nearer and nearer to Joshua. Finally Achan stood right in front of Joshua. God announced, "He is the guilty one." Now everyone knew! Achan could no longer hide his sin.

4. CONFESSION AND JUDGMENT
Joshua 7:19-26

Everybody stared at Achan. Quietly Joshua said, "My son, confess to God what you've done. Don't try to hide it any longer."

Achan answered, "I have sinned against the Lord God of Israel." Then he told Joshua exactly what he did.

Turning to some soldiers, Joshua ordered, "Go to Achan's tent! Bring the stolen goods here! Get all his possessions, his sheep, oxen, and everything he owns." How hard this was for Joshua! But he had no choice. He had to obey God.

The soldiers took Achan, everything he owned, and his *whole family* outside the camp. There they stoned them to death and burned them with fire.

Show Illustration #4

Then the people of Israel covered Achan and his family with a pile of stones. No one would ever forget what happened there!

Achan paid an awful price for his sin. So did his family. Achan caused Israel to lose a battle and 36 soldiers lost their lives. How many suffered because one man stole a few things for himself!

It is not pleasant to think about the anger of God. But it is important for us to understand that God hates sin.

What are some lessons you learned today? (Let students respond.)

1. "Be sure your sin will find you out" (Numbers 32:33).
2. For His [God's] eyes are upon the ways of man, and He sees all his goings (Proverbs 5:21). "God sees me" (Genesis 16:13). We can never hide anything from God.
3. "Trust in the Lord with all your heart; and lean not unto your own understanding" (Proverbs 3:5).
4. When we sin, others also suffer.

Will you confess to God (right now) any secret sin and ask His forgiveness?

(Remind your students of 1 John 1:9 and Proverbs 28:13. God does forgive the *guilt* of our sin when we confess it. But He may cause us to suffer the *consequences* of our sin.)

Lesson 2
FORGIVENESS AND VICTORY

Scripture to be studied: Joshua 8:1-35, Deuteronomy 27:1-26; 28:1-14

The *aim* of the lesson: To show that when sin is confessed and judged, God forgives and pardons (Psalm 103:12).

What your students should *know*: That God blesses and uses the forgiven sinner.

What your students should *feel*: The joy of forgiven sin.

What your students should *do*: Promise God that they will faithfully read His Word.

Lesson outline for the teacher's and students' notebooks:

1. God encourages Joshua (Joshua 8:1-2).
2. Joshua follows God's battle plan (Joshua 8:3-17).
3. God gives victory to Israel (Joshua 8:18-29).
4. Israel renews covenant with God (Joshua 8:30-35; Deuteronomy 27:1-26; 28:1-14).

The verse to be memorized:

Fear the LORD, and serve Him in sincerity and in truth.
(Joshua 24:14a)

NOTE TO THE TEACHER

Joshua 7 opens with a dark picture of the "anger of the Lord kindled against the children of Israel." Sin had broken Israel's fellowship with God. His power promised to them was interrupted. The picture brightens at the end of the chapter. For when the sin was confessed and judged, "the Lord turned from the fierceness of His anger."

God did not abandon the Israelites. He gave them another opportunity. This time Joshua and Israel obeyed God exactly. So they experienced His power and blessing again.

God does not want us to continue to be sad about our sin once we have confessed it to Him. (See Isaiah 12:1.) As with the Israelites, God provides forgiveness for us when we tell Him we have sinned and are sorry. (See Psalm 103:12; 1 John 1:7, 9.) He expects us to believe we are forgiven. Then we are to serve Him with joy and gladness (Philippians 3:13-14).

The Israelites learned (1) that God loved them even when He was angry; (2) that God does forgive; (3) that God's blessing begins again when sin is confessed. These are lessons your students should learn from Joshua 8.

THE LESSON

Mother had warned John many times: "You'll be punished if you ever climb the big shade tree out front." Mother loved John and she knew this was dangerous.

One day she saw John swaying back and forth in the uppermost branches. What do you think Mother did? (Let students make suggestions.) She ordered him to come down at once, spanked him, and made him sit inside for one hour. John deserved this punishment.

Do you think John's mother would forgive him for disobeying her? (Encourage response.) Of course she would. Later, John was genuinely sorry he had disobeyed. He promised his mother he'd never do that again and asked her forgiveness. She smiled and put her arm around him. "John," she said, "I love you and I don't want you to get hurt. You are forgiven. Now go out with your friends. I'll call you when it is time to help with the chores."

John hugged his mother and dashed outside. Their loving, happy relationship was restored. John was still his mother's son. She would continue ro love him, feed him, care for him, *and* punish him when he disobeyed.

It is the same in the family of God. When we sin He punishes us–sometimes severely. (See 1 Corinthians 11:27-31.) But He does not throw us out of His family. When we are genuinely sorry we have done wrong and ask Him to forgive us, He does. (See 1 John 1:9; Proverbs 28:13.) Our happy fellowship with God is renewed. He again uses us for Himself.

In our last lesson, we learned that the people of Israel were punished because of sin. (Review with questions. Emphasize (1) Achan's sin of stealing and God's severe punishment; (2) the Lord's judgment of Joshua when he failed to ask God's direction.)

God did not leave the Israelites. He did not remove Joshua as leader of His people. After punishing them for their sin, the Lord forgave them. (See Joshua 7:26.) Their fellowship with Him was restored. Now God's plans for Israel could continue.

1. GOD ENCOURAGES JOSHUA
Joshua 8:1-2

Show Illustration #5

The Lord God spoke to Joshua. "Don't be afraid, Joshua. Don't be discouraged!"

Why would this great leader be afraid and discouraged? (Stimulate discussion: *The defeat at Ai. Thirty-six soldiers killed in the battle. The news of the defeat known by everyone in Canaan. The tension of Achan's confession and death. The uncertainty of God's help in the days ahead. The uncertainty of Israel's future after their sin.*)

God knew what Joshua was thinking. He understood his doubts and fears. Now the Lord wanted Joshua to know that He had forgiven the Israelites for their sin. God wanted Joshua to believe that He was still with them and would make them victorious.

– 21 –

The Lord commanded, "Joshua, I want you to go up to Ai with *all* your soldiers."

How would this differ from the Israelites' first attack on Ai? (*The people of Israel thought they could conquer Ai with only a few soldiers!–Joshua 7:3.*)

Then God gave Joshua this wonderful promise: "I have given to you the king of Ai, the people, the city, and the land."

Joshua remembered what God had said before they marched around Jericho: "I've given to you Jericho, with its king and valiant warriors!" (See Joshua 6:2.) The Lord kept that promise so Joshua now had nothing to fear. The Lord God would be with him.

God continued, "I want you to destroy Ai and the king just as you destroyed Jericho. This time you may keep for yourselves the animals and all the possessions of the people."

Poor Achan! If he'd only waited, he could've had what he wanted!

The Bible does not say that Joshua questioned God. But he could have wondered, *Do You want us to march around Ai 13 times as we did at Jericho? Are You going to cause the walls to crumble?*

No! God had a different plan. This time they would go to war.

2. JOSHUA FOLLOWS GOD'S BATTLE PLAN
Joshua 8:3-17

Joshua certainly did not make his own decisions this time. Instead, he listened carefully as God explained how the battle could be won. Then he took charge of the army. He followed the Lord's plan exactly. First he chose 30,000 of his best soldiers.

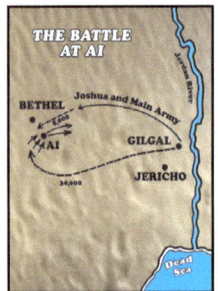

Show Illustration #6

(Indicate movements of army on map as you explain.)

"Under cover of darkness," Joshua commanded, "take your position west of Ai. Wait there until I give you the signal to enter the city." Giving full details, he added, "Be ready for action!"

While the people in Ai slept, 30,000 soldiers of Israel slipped silently into hiding as Joshua had ordered. Not one person in the city knew they were there.

Early the next morning Joshua and the rest of his men moved secretly to the north of Ai. That night he sent 5,000 soldiers to hide between Ai and Bethel. (These would protect the Israelite army if the army of Bethel came out to fight.) Joshua and the remaining soldiers shifted to the valley near Ai where they could be seen easily.

Early the next morning when the king of Ai arose, he blinked with amazement when he saw the Israelite army. Immediately he summoned his army, threw open the city gates, and rushed out with his men to defeat the Israelites as before. Every soldier joined in the battle. None stayed to guard the city. Proudly they shouted, "We defeated Israel before! We shall do it again!"

Ah, but things were different now. There was something the king of Ai did not know. What was it? (Encourage discussion. (1) *This time God was on the Israelites' side. He had promised to destroy Ai and give Israel the victory.* (2) *There were soldiers hidden outside the city.*)

Joshua and the soldiers ran from the army of Ai. They *pretended* they were being overtaken as before.

The soldiers of Ai shouted victoriously, "Look at them run! We're stronger than the Israelites! Chase them!" The Israelites rushed down the hillside followed hotly by the men of Ai.

3. GOD GIVES VICTORY TO ISRAEL
Joshua 8:18-29

Show Illustration #7

Right then, at God's command, Joshua spun fo around. Holding his spear high, he pointed toward Ai. This was the signal for which the hidden soldiers were waiting. They sprang from hiding and dashed into the city, setting it on fire. Billows of smoke rose to the sky. The terrified screams of women and children filled the air.

The Israelite soldiers who had been fleeing, turned and caught the army of Ai. There was no escape.

While Joshua kept his spear pointed to Ai, his army slew all the people. Seizing all the valuables and the cattle, the Israelite soldiers rushed from the city before it burned to the ground. God gave them complete victory. With His power, they were stronger than their enemies. As they returned to their camp, not one could boast of what *they* had done that day. Instead, they thanked God that *He* gave them the victory.

The Israelites knew they could *never* win their battles without God's help. How glad they were that God had not given up on them when they sinned! Instead He forgave them and continued to give them the land of Canaan as He promised.

Why do you think God arranged for these battle experiences of the Israelites at Ai to be recorded? (Let students respond. Read Romans 15:4) What should we learn from Israel's experience? (Encourage discussion. *(1) Even though fellowship with God is broken by sin, God forgives sin when it is confessed and fellowship is restored, I John 1:9; Proverbs 28:13; (2) God never forsakes His children, Hebrews 13:5c; [3] when the forgiven sinner obeys Him, God again uses him in His service.*)

4. ISRAEL RENEWS COVENANT WITH GOD
Joshua 8:30-35; Deuteronomy 27; 28:1-14

Jericho and Ai were a heap of ruins. The kings and all their people were dead. News of the power of the God of the Israelites spread rapidly throughout the whole land. The people of Canaan watched the people of Israel nervously. "Where will they attack next?" the Canaanites wondered fearfully.

Joshua led the whole company of Israelites almost fifty (50) kilometers north to Shechem. (Indicate on map.) Shechem was located in a valley between two mountains–Mount Ebal on the north and Mount Gerizim on the south. There would be no battle this time. Instead, Joshua was obeying God's command which Moses had given before he died. (See Deuteronomy 27.) He was going to lead the people in worshiping God.

The Israelites were made up of 12 tribes or family groups. Joshua spoke first to the leaders of six of the tribes. "Take everyone in your family groups," he commanded. "Stand on the slopes of Mount Gerizim. (Indicate on map.) When I read the blessings which God has promised if we obey Him, you will shout loudly 'AMEN' (So let it be)."

Turning to the leaders of the other six tribes Joshua ordered, "Climb the slopes of Mount Ebal with everyone in your tribes. (Indicate on map.) God will curse us with judgments if we disobey Him. On Mount Ebal I shall read the curses of which God has warned us. As I mention each one, you all shout loudly 'AMEN' (So let it be)."

The leaders of Israel stood in the valley beside the Ark of God. All the people watched as Joshua built an altar with stones. Then he took a male animal with no defects and sacrificed it on the altar as a burnt offering. This showed that the people of Israel renewed their dedication to God and consecrated themselves completely to do His will. Next Joshua killed another unblemished animal (without a flaw or defect) (Joshua 8:18-29) and sacrificed it on the altar as a peace offering. This was their sacrifice of thanksgiving to God for the victories He had given them.

Show Illustration #8

Then Joshua covered the stone altar with plaster and wrote on it a copy of the law of God. The Israelites were never to forget His law. They must always obey it.

Joshua began to read the blessings that God promised if they obeyed the law. After each one, the whole countryside resounded with a thunderous "AMEN" from Mount Gerizim. Then he read the cursings. Again there was a resounding "AMEN"–this time from Mount Ebal.

(*Teacher:* Divide your class into two groups. Read a few of the blessings from Deuteronomy 28. Let one group say "Amen" loudly. Read some of the cursings from Deuteronomy 27. Let the second group say "Amen.")

Do you know why God commanded Joshua to do this? *(1) He wanted the people of Israel to understand how important His Word is; (2) He wanted everyone in Israel to know what His Word says; (3) He wanted the Israelites to know they had a choice to make–to obey or disobey His commands. And what would happen to them depended on their choice.*

(*Teacher:* Read Romans 15:4 again. Encourage the students to suggest reasons why God had this incident recorded for us.)

(1) God wants *everyone* to *know* His Word, the Bible. (2) He wants everyone to obey His Word. (3) He wants everyone to enjoy the blessings and victories which result from obedience to His Word. (4) He also wants us to know the punishment He promises for rejecting His Word. (See John 3:36.)

Do you read God's Word daily? Do you ask Him to speak to you in a special way from His Word each time you read it? God's Word is a lamp to our feet and a light to our path. (See Psalm 119:105.) You can only know His direction for your life as you learn from the Word of God.

Lesson 3
PRAYERLESSNESS AND WRONG DECISIONS

Scripture to be studied: Joshua 9:1-27; 10:1-43

The *aim* of the lesson: To show the importance of prayer before making decisions.

What your students should *know*: That failure to ask God's guidance often results in wrong decisions which bring problems to our lives.

What your students should *feel*: Inadequacy to make right decisions without God's help.

What your students should *do*: Determine to seek God's guidance prayerfully in every decision they make.

Lesson outline for the teacher's and students' notebooks:
1. The trickery of the Gibeonites (Joshua 9:3-5, 24).
2. The neglect of the Israelites (Joshua 9:6-27).
3. Involvement in Gibeonite war (Joshua 10:1-9).
4. Victory through God's miraculous help (Joshua 10:10-43; Psalm 115:1).

The verse to be memorized:
Fear the LORD, and serve Him in sincerity and in truth.
(Joshua 24:14a)

THE LESSON

For a few moments, let us pretend we are GIBEONITES. (*Teacher:* Write the word *Gibeonites* on the chalkboard or on a large card to hold before the class.) Are you wondering, *Who are the Gibeonites?* They were people who lived in the city of Gibeon. (Have student indicate Gibeon on back cover map. Observe its nearness to Jericho and Ai.)

If we had lived in Gibeon in the time of Joshua, what news would we have heard in our city? (Let students respond. Review briefly the conquest of Jericho and the battles at Ai.)

How do you think we would have felt? (Allow response.) There are three facts we would know because of what we heard: (1) God promised to give the Israelites our land. (2) God commanded we should be destroyed (9:24). (3) God told the Israelites they could make peace agreements with nations far away from their borders (Deuteronomy 20:10-20).

> **NOTE TO THE TEACHER**
> God commands us to pray without ceasing (1 Thessalonians 5:17). He promises to give us wisdom to make right decisions if we will ask Him (Proverbs 3:5-6; Psalm 32:8; James 1:8). But Satan–our enemy–does not want us to pray. If he can succeed in keeping us from praying, he has gained a victory in our lives. When we forget to pray, we often make wrong decisions. In this way Satan turns us aside from the total obedience to God.
>
> James 4:7-8 tells us how to overcome our powerful enemy. We draw near to God through (1) daily fellowship with Him in reading His Word and (2) continually depending on Him through prayer.
>
> God is more powerful than Satan, our enemy. (see 1 John 4:4.) And we can have his power. Do not fail to use to use it.
>
> Depending upon the ages and abilities of your students, this lesson can be enacted.

We had better have a meeting and decide what we are going to do to protect ourselves. What do you suggest? (Allow class to make numerous suggestions.)

1. THE TRICKERY OF THE GIBEONITES
Joshua 9:3-5, 24

Show Illustration #9

As the leaders in Gibeon (back in Joshua's day) met together, they agreed they did not want to be killed. They did not want their city to be destroyed. They tried hard to think of a way to protect themselves.

"If we could make the Israelites decide to be our friends, they would not fight us," one leader suggested.

– 23 –

Another asked, "But how can we do that? Their God has commanded them not to make friends with any of the people living here!"

I have a good idea," said a third. "Let's fool them. They will make a peace agreement with us if we can convince them that we live far away."

But how can we get the Israelites to believe that?" others wanted to know.

What suggestions would you have offered if you had been in that meeting? (Let students give ideas.)

Listen to the ideas the Gibeonites had. (Read Joshua 9:3-5 slowly.) What are they going to do? (Let students describe the Gibeonites' plan.) Do you think Joshua and the Israelites will be fooled?

2. THE NEGLECT OF THE ISRAELITES
Joshua 9:6-27

Now let us move over to Gilgal where the people of Israel are encamped. (Show on map. Review what happened there when they first crossed the Jordan River, Joshua 4:1-18. See Old Testament Volume 16, Lesson 3.)

The pillar of stones at Gilgal reminded the Israelites that God had dried up the Jordan so they could cross over on dry land. It also reminded them that they served the living and powerful God who was strong enough to defeat their enemies.

Today something different is happening in the camp. Strangers have arrived. Who are they? Why have they come? Let us go over to hear what they are saying to Joshua and the leaders of Israel.

Show Illustration #10

"We have come from a distant land," they announced. "We have heard about your God. We would like to make peace with you."

The Israelite leaders immediately replied, "How do we know you do not live nearby? If you do, we cannot make peace with you."

"We'll be your servants," answered the strangers.

"But who are you?" demanded Joshua. "From where do you come? How can we know that you came from a distant land?"

"Look at our bread," they answered. "We took it hot out of the ovens when we left home. Now it is hard and moldy. Look at our clothes. They were new. Now they are worn out because of our long trip. Look at our wine skins. They were new when we left home. Now they are torn. Our journey has been long and tiring," they sighed.

If you could whisper to Joshua, what would you like to tell him? (Let students answer.)

I would like to call him aside and say, "Joshua, before you make any decision, be sure to talk to God about it. He knows whether or not these people are telling the truth. He knows where they live. Ask Him if you should make peace with them. Do not rely on your own wisdom!"

But listen to this sad verse in the Bible. (*Teacher:* Read Joshua 9:14. *Joshua and the leaders forgot to pray*.)

Instead, they tasted the wine and bread to check the story of their visitors. Nodding their heads in agreement, Joshua and the others believed these men had come from a faraway place. And they made peace with them. Think of it! They made peace with the Gibeonites who lied, saying they lived far off–not close by.

Because Joshua did not pray, he made the WRONG decision. (*Teacher:* Read Deuteronomy 20:16-17; Exodus 23:31b-33 slowly. Read several times if necessary.)

God had said, "The people who live in and around Canaan must die. Do not make any agreements with them!"

But Joshua, who had been deceived, said, "Let these strangers live. Make peace with them!"

For several reasons God wanted the Israelites to destroy all the people around them: (1) God had to judge them because they rejected Him and willfully sinned (Deuteronomy 8:20; 12:31). (2) They bowed down to idols refusing to trust and worship the true and living God. (3) They lived wicked lives (Deuteronomy 9:4-5). (4) They would influence the Israelites to worship their false make-believe gods and become as wicked and sinful as they were (Deuteronomy 29:18).

The Gibeonites returned home happily. "We fooled them!" they exclaimed. "We won't be killed. Our cities will not be destroyed! The Israelites made peace with us!"

Three days later, Joshua and his men discovered they had been tricked. They realized they had made a wrong decision. But it was too late.

Joshua called for the Gibeonites, asking, "Why did you lie to us to make us believe you lived far away?"

They answered, "We were afraid of you. We heard about your powerful God. We wanted to save our lives."

"God expects us to keep our promise," said Joshua. "We shall not kill you. But from now on you will be our slaves. You will cut wood for us and carry our water."

As a consequence of Israel's wrong decision, they could not destroy the deceitful Gibeonites. Instead, they would have to live among them.

3. INVOLVEMENT IN THE GIBEONITE WAR
Joshua 10:1-9

Joshua was soon to experience another consequence of his wrong decision.

When the king of Jerusalem (indicate on map) heard that the Gibeonites had made peace with the Israelites, he was really frightened. Gibeon, he new, was a great city. And the Gibeonites were mighty men. So he knew that his city (Jerusalem) would be defeated when Joshua attacked it.

He had a plan. Sending messengers to four other strong cities he asked, "Will you help me fight against Gibeon? If we join together we can defeat the Gibeonites."

Show Illustration #11

Without delay the armies from Jerusalem and these four cities marched to Gibeon. They set up their camps all around the city ready for battle.

The Gibeonites knew they were not strong enough to fight against five armies. So they sent a message to Joshua immediately. "Help! Help! Come quickly. All our enemies are fighting against us. We shall be destroyed if you do not come immediately!"

The Bible does not tell us what Joshua thought when he got this message. But it could have been like this: *Why did I ever promise to protect the Gibeonites instead of killing them? If only I had prayed to God before I made that wrong decision. How are we ever going to conquer five armies at once? I had hoped to fight them one at a time!*

This time Joshua did remember to pray. God knew how frightened Joshua was. To encourage him, the Lord said, "Do not be afraid, Joshua. I have already given you the victory. Not one of those men will be able to stand against you!"

How do you think Joshua felt when he heard this? (*Discuss.*) He did not know *how* God was going to give him the victory. But he *knew* God would do as He promised.

This time Joshua made the right decision. He believed God and prepared for battle. That night, Joshua and his army attacked the enemy soldiers while they slept. Bewildered, the sleepy men stumbled to their feet and ran.

4. VICTORY THROUGH GOD'S MIRACULOUS HELP
Joshua 10:10-43; Psalm 115:1

Joshua's soldiers chased them, killing many with their swords.

Show Illustration #12

Suddenly God sent a hailstorm on the enemy's armies. And more soldiers were killed by hail than by the swords of Israel. But not one hailstone hit the Israelite army!

The battle raged all day. Night was coming. Joshua did not want any of these wicked people to escape. So he spoke to God before all the Israelites. "O God," he prayed, "make the sun and moon stand still until all our enemies are killed!"

Do you think God answered Joshua's prayer? Let's read what He says in His Word. (*Read Joshua 10:13-14.*) What a difference it made when Joshua remembered to pray! Now he was doing things God's way. And God performed miracles for him.

The five kings saw they were losing the battle, so they hid in a cave. But Joshua dragged them out and killed them. Because Joshua knew God helped the Israelites to win the battle, he gave glory to Him. And his soldiers were encouraged when Joshua reminded them: "The Lord will defeat all our enemies."

(*Read Romans 15:4.*) What does God want us ro learn from this experience in Joshua's life? (*Allow response, leading students to understand that we have an enemy who does not want us to obey God.*) Who is our enemy? (*Satan, who wants us to make a peace agreement with him.*) (*Read 2 Corinthians 11:14.*) Many times we do not recognize Satan, just as Joshua did not recognize his enemy.

How important it is for us to ask God for wisdom in each decision we make! (*Read Proverbs 3:5-6.*) Will you determine that from now on you will seek the Lord's guidance before you make any decisions?

Lesson 4
RECEIVING GOD'S PROVISIONS

Scripture to be studied: Joshua 12:1-24:33

The *aim* of the lesson: To show that God provided for the Israelites just as He had promised.

What your students should *know*: That God provides all that His children need today in order to live victorious Christian lives.

What your students should *feel*: A desire to receive and use all that God is willing to provide for them.

What your students should *do*: Believe God's promises and claim them.

Lesson outline for the teacher's and students' notebooks:
1. A place to live (Joshua 11:23; 13:1-33; 15:1-19:51; 21:1-45).
2. A place of safety (Joshua 20:1-9; Numbers 35:11-16).
3. Freedom from fear (Joshua 14:1-15).
4. Courage to stand true (Joshua 23:1-24:33).

The verse to be memorized:

Fear the LORD, and serve Him in sincerity and in truth.
(Joshua 24:14a)

NOTE TO THE TEACHER

You will want to make it clear to your students that God guides us through: (1) His Word; (2) the advice of a godly person–our pastors or Christian parents; (3) circumstances; or (4) uneasiness when a wrong decision is made.

THE LESSON

What do families provide for their children? (*Food, clothing, home, education, medicine, etc.*) God has a family *today* for whom He provides. Who belongs to His family? (*All who trust in Jesus Christ as Saviour.*) God loves to provide for His own. This is true today. It was true in the long, long ago when Joshua lived.

Joshua led the people of Israel across the Jordan River into Canaan. During the seven years which followed, Joshua and his army conquered one city after another. Each city was a little kingdom. (Review briefly the incidents of Jericho, Ai, Gibeon, and the war against the five kings. Point out that there were many more cities and more battles. See Joshua 12.) Why did God command Joshua to destroy all the cities in Canaan? (Review reasons given in Lesson 3, point 2.)

1. A PLACE TO LIVE
Joshua 11:23; 13:1-33; 15:1-19:51; 21:1-45

The Lord spoke to Joshua saying, "You are getting old. Before you die, I want you to divide this land among the tribes of Israel. I am going to provide each family group with a section of the land in which to live. None will be left out."

Joshua wondered, *How can I know which section should be given to each tribe?*

Before he could ask, God continued, "Divide the land by casting a lot. I shall make the choice for each tribe." (See Joshua 13:6-7; 14:1-2.)

The Bible does not tell us how Joshua cast the lot. But Jewish custom suggests that the name of each tribe was placed in an urn or pot. Descriptions of portions of the land were placed in another pot. Then Joshua and the leaders drew a name and a description at the same time.

Show Illustration #13

God, who knows all things and can do anything, matched the tribe with the piece of land as He had planned. Any who might be dissatisfied could not blame Joshua. It was God who chose the places they were to live. The Lord knew what was best for each family group. The size of the territory agreed with the size of the tribe.

(*Teacher:* Note that two-and-one-half tribes received their land on the east side of the Jordan River and weren't included in this distribution. See Joshua 14:3. Observe that Ephraim and Manasseh, Joseph's two sons, received his share of the land. See Joshua 16:4. As we will see, the tribe of Levi didn't receive a portion.)

What do we do with our land? some of the leaders wondered.

Joshua explained God's plan. "If any enemies are in your land, you must chase them out completely. God will help you (Joshua 13:6). Then you are to build houses and plant gardens. Your wandering and fighting are over. You may settle down and enjoy the land. The Lord has provided it for you." How happy the Israelites were!

One tribe–the tribe of Levi–received something special. What do you remember about the Levites? (Review Numbers 1:47-54; 3:1-4:49; 8:1-26, Old Testament Volume 13, Lesson 2.)

God explained to Joshua His reason for honoring the Levites. "These are My servants," He said. "I have appointed them to take care of My tabernacle at Shiloh. (Use map– illustration 13–to point out that the tabernacle was located in the *center* of the land. The lives of God's people were to revolve around worship of Him.) The Levites are the only ones who may come near the place where I meet with My people." (See Numbers 18:21-22.) What an honor to be chosen by the Lord for such a responsibility!

God continued, "Unlike the other tribes, the Levites will not have time to farm the land. They will give all their time to My service. They will not receive a portion of land. Instead, I want each tribe to give to the Levites cities in which to live and land for their animals." (See Numbers 35:1-5; Joshua 21:1-45.)

The Levites were given 48 cities. They also received one-tenth of the harvest from all the fields. When the people brought sacrifices to the tabernacle, one-tenth was given to the Levites (Numbers 18:20-32).

God promised the Levites that He Himself would take care of all their needs (Joshua 13:14, 33). Each family received from the Lord a selected place in which to live. Just so, He has chosen specific places for you and me. He chose the land in which we were born. He placed us in this city (or village). And God has a special purpose for each of us (Ephesians 1:1-12).

God gives some the honor of being pastors or teachers or missionaries who serve Him with all their time as did the Levites. Those who do other kinds of work have the privilege of supporting God's full-time servants.

Do you thank God for setting you in the place of His choosing? Do you live for His glory in this place? (See Ephesians 1:12.)

2. A PLACE OF SAFETY
Joshua 20:1-9; Numbers 35:11-16

Six of the 48 cities given to the Levites were to be used for a special purpose. (See Joshua 20:7-8.) They were called "cities of refuge." (Point to the cities on map, illustration #13: Kedesh-Naphtali, Shechem, Kirjath-arba, Bezer, Ramoth, Golan.) A refuge is a *place of safety*.

God knew that sometimes accidents would happen. He planned the six cities of refuge as places of safety for any who might *accidentally* kill someone. (See Deuteronomy 19:4-6.)

Show Illustration #14

If a person *accidentally* killed someone he was to run as fast as he could to the closest city of refuge. There he must tell the Levites about the accident. The Levites decided whether or not the man was telling the truth. If they agreed he had not killed the person *on purpose*, they would say to him, "You may stay here in this city of refuge. You'll be safe as long as you stay *in the city*. No one may touch you here. If you leave the city, you'll no longer be protected." Everyone knew that to be outside the refuge city meant death. For a relative of the dead person would try to kill the one responsible for the accident. The refugee knew he had to remain inside the city until the High Priest died. Only then could he return home without fear of being killed.

These cities did *not* protect anyone who killed someone else on purpose. Such a person had to die. (See Exodus 21:12; Deuteronomy 19:11-13.)

There are four facts to be remembered about the six cities of refuge:

1. They could be reached by everyone (Indicate on map.)
2. They were open to anyone.
3. The gates were never locked.
4. They were the only places of safety for the guilty.

(*Teacher:* Explain that they were guilty even though they killed unintentionally.)

If innocent people needed a place of refuge, how much more do we, who purposely sin, need a refuge!

God loved us so much that He provided a perfect *place of safety* for us. Our Refuge is the Lord Jesus Christ (Hebrews 6:18).

1. Jesus Christ is available to ALL (John 3:16).
2. The way to Him is never closed. He receives ALL who come to Him at any time (Revelation 22:17).
3. There is absolute safety in Christ (John 6:37; 10:27-29).
4. He is the ONLY place of safety or refuge (Hebrews 10:28-31; John 14:6).

If you have never done so, will you right now ask the Lord Jesus to be your Refuge from the punishment of sin? When your trust is in Him, you have eternal life and are safe forever. (See John 10:28-29.)

3. FREEDOM FROM FEAR
Joshua 14:1-15

When we are certain of eternal life in Heaven, we have nothing of which to be afraid here on earth. Do you remember Caleb? (Review briefly the account of the spies in Numbers 13 and 14. See Old Testament Volume 13, Lesson 4.) Caleb was

40 years old when he went with 11 men to spy out the land of Canaan. Ten of the spies were afraid and reported that the people should not enter the land God had promised them. But Caleb was *not* afraid because he wholly followed the Lord God.

Caleb had agreed, "Yes, there are giants in the land. They are stronger than we are. BUT we do not need to fear. *God has promised to give us the land–and He will!*" (Recall with the students that all the Israelites above age 20, except Caleb and Joshua, died in the wilderness because they were afraid and refused to trust God.)

Years later when the people of Israel were settling in Canaan, Caleb was 85 years old. Standing before Joshua one day, he made a special request. "Joshua, do you remember what God promised me 45 years ago? He said I could have the land I walked over when we spied out the land. I would like to have the mountain region of Hebron. (Indicate on map, illustration 13.) I know there are giants there–giants who are strong and fierce. But I am not afraid."

Joshua thought about Caleb's request. He remembered the day that together the two had brought back a good report of the land. Gladly then Joshua gave Hebron to Caleb.

Show Illustration #15

And Caleb, completely trusting God, chased out the giants who were living in Hebron (Joshua 15:14). Why was old Caleb brave? (*Because he trusted God*)

Are you ever afraid? (Let students give suggestions of their fears.) These are "giants" which frighten us. But God does not want us to be tormented by fear. "Behold, God is my salvation; I will trust and not be afraid" (Isaiah 12:2). (Read slowly and distinctly Isaiah 41:13; Hebrews 13:16; and Psalm 56:3.) The next time you are scared, remember these promises and trust God as Caleb did. God does not want you to have a fearful spirit. (See 2 Timothy 1:7.) Let Him defeat whatever giant makes you afraid. Caleb believed God. Do you?

4. COURAGE TO STAND TRUE
Joshua 23:1-24:33

When Joshua was 110 years old, he knew he would soon die. How he loved the people of Israel! He longed that they would obey God. Once more he wanted to remind them of what God commanded.

Show Illustration #16

Calling the leaders together, he challenged them again to remember all God had done for them. (*Teacher:* Use questions to review briefly the history recorded in Joshua 24:1-13.) "God has kept every promise," Joshua emphasized (Joshua 23:14). "We never could have had this land if He had not helped us" (Joshua 23:9; 24:13).

Looking serious, Joshua gave them a challenge. "Today you must make a choice. Are you going to serve God or idols? You cannot serve both. I have made my choice. All in my house are going to serve the living Lord!"

The people all answered quickly, "We, too, shall serve the living God."

"Do you realize what you are promising?" Joshua asked. "God is holy. He is jealous. He will not share your worship and your loyalty with false gods and idols. God will provide the courage for you to stand true to Him if you will obey Him."

"What must we do?" asked the leaders.

Joshua explained clearly:

"(1) Obey the law of God completely. This means you must know His law, think about it, and do it. (See Joshua 23:6. Indicate illustrations at top of page 16.)

"(2) Separate yourselves from those who do not belong to the Lord God. Never marry anyone who does not serve the living, true God. Do not even mention the names of their false gods (Joshua 23:7, 12). Destroy any idols you have (Joshua 24:23).

"(3) Love the Lord God (Joshua 23:8, 11). He has done many marvelous things for you. You can show your gratitude by worshiping Him and loving Him."

Joshua reminded them that God would bless them if they obeyed Him. But he also warned that disobedience would result in God's judgment.

Suppose Joshua were standing here right now saying, "Choose you today whom you will serve!" How would you respond? Whom would *you* choose to serve? God? Or Satan? (See Matthew 6:24.)

God is willing to provide all the courage you need to stand true to Him.

1. You have His word, the Bible. If you study and obey it, your great enemy, Satan, will not have control over you.
2. Do not be like unbelievers around you. God challenges you to be like His Son, Jesus Christ (Romans 12:1-2). You must never marry someone who is not a Christian.
3. He challenges you to love Him (Matthew 22:37-39).

If you obey Him, He will give you courage to do even what is difficult. He gives courage to tell others about Jesus, though they may laugh and refuse to believe. He will give you courage to say "no" when Satan tempts you to sin.

Let us thank God for all He has provided for us.

NOTE TO THE TEACHER

It took the Israelites seven years to conquer the land of Canaan. With God's help, Joshua and his army destroyed one city after another, slaying the people "as Jehovah, the God of Israel, commanded." (See Joshua 10:40; 11:20, 23; Psalm 44:1-3.)

Forty-seven years after leaving Egypt, the people of Israel were settled in their land. As God had promised, He provided a portion of land for each tribe. He gave His people power to drive out the enemy.

God provides for His children today through Christ Jesus who conquered our enemy, Satan. (See Ephesians 1:15-23; Colossians 2:14-15.) We need to accept and use these provisions personally in order to enjoy the Christian life and live for the glory of God.

www.ingramcontent.com/pod-product-compliance
Lightning Source LLC
Chambersburg PA
CBHW060803090426
42736CB00002B/141